EDGE BOOKS

Unusual and Awesome

JOBS

Using

SCIENCE

Food Taster,
Human Lie Detector,
and More

by Jennifer Wendinger

CAPSTONE PRESS
a capstone imprint

Edge Books are published by Capstone Press,
1710 Roe Crest Drive, North Mankato, Minnesota 56003
www.capstonepub.com

Library of Congress Cataloging-in-Publication Data
Wendinger, Jennifer, author.
  Unusual and awesome jobs using science : Hollywood animal trainer, cave diver, and more /
by Jennifer Wendinger.
  pages cm. -- (You get paid for THAT?)
  Includes bibliographical references and index.
ISBN 978-1-4914-2031-7 (Hardcover)
ISBN 978-1-4914-2202-1 (e-Book PDF)
1. Science--Vocational guidance--Juvenile literature. 2. Scientists--Juvenile literature. 3.
Occupations--Juvenile literature. I. Title.
  Q147.W417 2015
  502.3--dc23
                        2014040361ISBN 978-1-4914-2031-7

Editorial Credits
Editor: Nate LeBoutillier
Designer: Veronica Scott
Media researcher: Jo Miller
Production specialist: Tori Abraham

Photo Credits
Alamy: MGM/RGA/Ronald Grant Archive, 12-13, Superstock/RGB, Ventures/Karen
Kasmauski, 25; Glow Images: Corbis RF, 17; Landov: EPA/Franziska Kraufmann, 4 (inset),
Reuters/Alex Grimm, 29; Newscom: Danita Delimont Photography/Scott T.Smith, 15,
PacificCoastNews, Juan Sharma, 11; Science Source: Alexis Rosenfeld, 7, Jim Reed, 23,
Philippe Garo, 19, Stephen & Donna O'Meara, 27; Shutterstock: Dray van Beeck, 8-9, Fisun
Ivan, 20, Marcus Bay, cover, solarseven, cover (background); SuperStock: Aurora Open, 4-5

Printed in the United States of America in Stevens Point, Wisconsin
042015   008940R

TABLE OF CONTENTS

BEYOND THE LAB

When you think of science jobs, do you think of long white coats and bubbling test tubes? Science careers don't always have to take place in a laboratory.

The following jobs show how people use science in unusual ways to make money. Some jobs, like professional food tasting and beard growing, explain how food science works. Others, like animal training and human lie detection, show how behavioral science is useful. You'll see just how unique, challenging, and downright adventurous a career in science can be.

Above: An adventure guide points out sites near Chamonix, France.
Left: A bearder shows his unusual facial hair design.

CAVE DIVER

HELP WANTED

special skills: swim 60 feet (18 meters) under water on one breath of air

education: cave diving certification

prior experience: must have completed more than 100 dives

hourly schedule: work hours vary and may require travel

salary: diver sets pay rate

A team of cave divers puts on scuba gear. The divers prepare to jump in a hole of water no bigger than a small pond. The divers know the water is deep and can stretch hundreds of feet below. They are preparing to jump in a **blue hole**.

Blue holes are underwater caves. Long ago blue holes were on dry land. Some looked like rocky cliffs. Birds nested there, and other animals made homes in the cliffs. Then the Ice Age came and froze over the land. When the ice melted, sea levels rose and filled up the cliffs like cups of water.

Some cave divers who explore blue holes are underwater **archaeologists**. They dive in the dark, murky caves for ancient **artifacts**. They search for things like bones, tools, and pottery.

---

blue hole—an underwater cave

archaeologist—a person who learns about the past by digging up old buildings or objects and studying them

artifact—an object made by human beings, especially a tool or weapon used in the past

extinct—no longer living; an extinct animal is one that has died out, with no more of its kind

When an artifact is found, team members record its location. Then divers make many dangerous dives back to the site. The divers gather every bone of every skeleton. They collect other material for testing too. On a dive near Mexico, divers collected bat droppings found near a human skeleton. Later the droppings helped scientists determine that the skeleton was more than 12,000 years old.

Underwater caves have very little oxygen. The low oxygen level keeps the artifacts in good condition. Divers know bringing artifacts to the surface can be tricky work. They realize certain artifacts, such as pottery, can be damaged by air. The divers take special care to preserve the artifacts they find. They know their work helps tell the story of how people lived thousands of years ago.

A cave diver explores the watery depths, where rare artifacts can be discovered at any moment.

HOLLYWOOD ANIMAL TRAINER

HELP WANTED

In 1943 a dog named Pal landed the starring role in *Lassie*. But Pal had help with a Hollywood animal trainer by his side. Hollywood animal trainers are people who work with animals to help them perform in movies. Some of these animals may also appear in TV shows or commercials.

Trainers usually work with one kind of animal. They might train **domestic** animals, such as cats. Or they might choose more **exotic** animals, like tigers. Trainers become experts by focusing on one type of animal. They learn how to read the animal's mood. They know when it's a good time to teach a trick and when it's not. This understanding helps the animal build trust. Trust keeps both the animal and trainer safe.

domestic—living near or with human beings
exotic—very different or unusual

Trainers work with a grizzly bear on the set of the movie
We Bought a Zoo.

Training animals can be very dangerous. In 2008 a young bear named Rocky was being trained to wrestle in movies. Rocky attacked and killed one of his trainers, Stephan Miller. A fellow trainer was able to get the bear off of Miller within seconds, but the bite and claw wounds proved fatal.

Actor and animal meet on the set of *Flipper*.

A scientific background in **biology** is very helpful when training animals. The dolphins that starred in the 1960s TV show *Flipper* had trainers who knew how to do more than teach tricks. The trainers knew how to balance the tank's salt level so the dolphins wouldn't get sick. They also knew how to reward the dolphins without overfeeding them. It was important for the trainers to understand how to care for the dolphins. Good health helped the animals learn tricks.

Whether they are working with dolphins or a pet like Pal, Hollywood animal trainers are hard workers. They care for their animals both on and off set. Their dedication can make this type of work an around-the-clock job.

biology—the study of plant and animal life

ADVENTURE GUIDE

HELP WANTED

special skills: good communication skills, physically fit and healthy

education: first aid, special knowledge of environment

prior experience: If experience is lacking, some places will train

hourly schedule: work hours vary; some trips can last weeks

salary: between $2,000 and $3,000 per month

For some Mother Nature is the best boss. These people prefer to take a canoe to work, not a car. They like to carry a backpack, not a briefcase. They enjoy teaching outside, not inside.

Being an adventure guide is an ideal job for this type of person. An adventure guide is not a typical tour guide. Depending on their skills, some guides take people rock climbing. Other guides take groups camping in the wilderness or rafting the waters of a roaring canyon. Some guides even travel to faraway places. These guides might give tours to people on safaris or in jungles.

Adventure guides use knowledge about biology to do their job. Some guides use their knowledge to educate their groups. They might point out a harmful plant or explain a certain birdcall. Others use their knowledge to help keep wildlife and plants safe. These guides are called **conservationists**.

conservationist—someone who works to protect Earth's natural resources

Some safari guides in Africa are conservationists. Part of their job is to protect animals and their **habitats**. They work against people who illegally hunt animals for their fur or tusks. This type of hunting can cause an animal to become **endangered**, or even worse, become extinct.

There is some risk—even the risk of death—involved with being an adventure guide. That's why the most skilled guides are educated ones. They do research to make sure the tours they lead are safe and fun.

habitat—the natural place and conditions in which a plant or animal lives
endangered—at risk of dying out

FOOD TASTER

special skills: keen sense of smell and taste; ability to describe how food tastes

education: degree in food science is very helpful

prior experience: other jobs involving tasting or description helpful

hourly schedule: some work days can be as short as two hours

salary: beginning around $29,000 per year

Roman leaders had food tasters thousands of years ago. The food taster's job was to try the leaders' meals in order to see if they were poisoned. If the tasters became sick or died after trying the food, the leaders knew the food had been poisoned.

Back then a food taster's job was to protect the leaders. Today tasters play a much different role. They make sure foods taste right before they go to market.

Many tasters have a degree in food science. Their degrees help them recommend alternate ingredients such as vitamins and minerals in addition to sugar and **food additives**. That's how sugary cereals, fruit snacks, or granola bars can taste good and still have nutritional value.

Food tasters try all kinds of foods. Some get paid to sample chocolate and ice cream. Others get paid to try less yummy things—even dog food.

food additive—a substance added to food to enhance its flavor or appearance

Professional coffee tasters sample the product.

PROFESSIONAL SLEEPER

special skills: able to fall asleep as needed and follow the rules of the project

education: study of sleep disorders very helpful

prior experience: previous participation in other scientific studies and understanding of sleep disorders is useful

schedule: hours vary by project

salary: pay varies by project but may be as high as $18,000 per study

Getting caught sleeping on the job is usually a bad thing. But sometimes it can be a good thing. And sometimes it can be a way of earning extra money.

A sleeper's job is to be scientifically studied while he or she sleeps. The sleepers allow researchers to study their brain waves and sleep patterns. If the sleeper can answer scientific questions and describe his or her sleep, scientists can learn a great deal. The information might help scientists understand why people dream or have **sleep disorders**.

Sleep disorders vary. Some people have sleep apnea, where sleep is constantly interrupted. Others may have a problem with sleepwalking or with insomnia, which prevents people from falling asleep. People with sleep disorders usually participate in studies to help scientists find solutions to their problems. They tend to care more about finding answers than making money.

sleep disorder—a disturbance of the normal sleep pattern

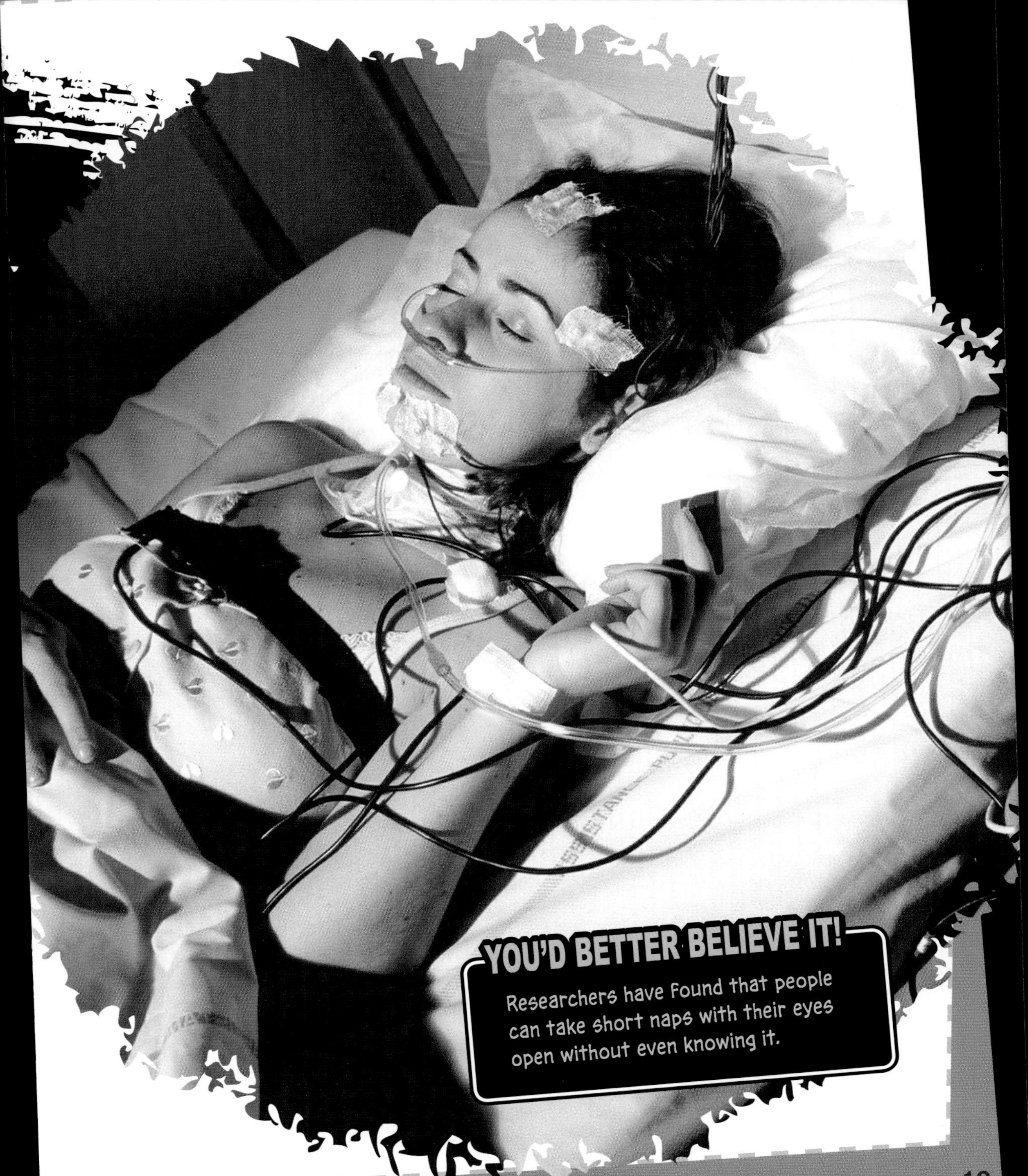

YOU'D BETTER BELIEVE IT!

Researchers have found that people can take short naps with their eyes open without even knowing it.

HUMAN LIE DETECTOR

special skills: critical thinking, good questioning skills

education: degree in criminal justice

prior experience: psychology training is a bonus

schedule: work hours vary; may include evening or night shifts

salary: police detectives make an average of $68,000 a year

When crimes are committed, **suspects** are brought in for questioning. Special police detectives study suspects to gather clues. As they ask the suspects questions, they watch suspects very carefully. They are looking for clues that suspects are telling the truth or lying. The information they gather can make a vital difference between solving a case or not.

The police detective is acting as a human lie detector. Detectives know about scientific research proving that when people tell lies their bodies behave differently. They sweat. Their pulses race. They squirm. Their eyes give clues when they dart or when the pupils grow larger or smaller. Their muscles can tense up and tighten around vocal cords, causing voices to become higher or squeakier than normal.

Not all people behave the same when they lie. Detectives still need solid **evidence** to arrest somebody for a crime. Reading body language is only a tool to help detectives do their jobs.

YOU'D BETTER BELIEVE IT!

As of today there is no machine or person able to detect lies 100 percent accurately.

suspect—a person who is thought to be guilty of a crime
evidence—information, items, and facts that help prove something to be true or false

STORM CHASER

special skills: observing and predicting weather patterns
education: degree in meteorology is helpful, but can be self-taught
prior experience: scientific study of weather and weather patterns
hourly schedule: seasonal work, typically during the spring
salary: most chasers earn money from the sale of data, photos, or videos

A couple of storm chasers are parked on a gravel road in the countryside. They videotape a dark, hanging cloud. They know by its formation that it's a funnel cloud. They know at any moment the cloud could drop into a spinning tornado of destruction.

Even before storms hit the ground, storm chasers spring into action. They race along the outskirts of storms. They observe, record, and gather data.

Meteorologists make the most skilled storm chasers. Meteorologists study weather for a living. They release weather balloons into the **atmosphere**. The balloons carry scientific equipment that sends data back down to earth. The balloons allow the meteorologists to predict bad weather days ahead of time.

Storm chasers use **tornado probes** and **radar**. They drive special vehicles designed for storm chasing. Chasers know the work they do is dangerous. Every year a few chasers die in pursuit of deadly storms.

Chasers record data on a developing storm.

A truck equipped with radar is ready to chase.

meteorologist—a person who studies and predicts the weather

atmosphere—the mixture of gases that surrounds the Earth

tornado probe—a portable weather station that collects tornado data where other instruments can't

radar—a device that uses radio waves to track the locations of objects

23

LAUGHTER THERAPIST

special skills: sense of humor and understanding of human behavior

education: background in science, counseling, or the arts is helpful

prior experience: experience with human behavioral studies is useful

hourly schedule: usually done as part-time work

salary: average of $26,000 per year

There's an old saying that laughter is the best medicine. Some scientists have found this to be quite true.

Studies show that laughter reduces stress. Laughter also releases **endorphins** into the blood stream and increases the body's output of **serotonin**, which makes people feel better. When someone has been sick for a long time, they laugh less. Their bodies miss out on a natural way to feel better.

Laughter therapists use techniques to make their patients vibrate with laughter. This laughter makes the patient relax and feel less pain.

Laughter therapists do not try to cure sick people. Instead doctors use laughter therapists to help their patients feel less stress. They believe that the more patients laugh, the better they will feel.

endorphin—a chemical released by the brain that masks pain and triggers positive feelings
serotonin—a chemical created by the human body that is responsible for maintaining mood balance

YOU'D BETTER BELIEVE IT!

Children laugh an average of 400 times a day while adults laugh an average of 15.

VOLCANOLOGIST

special skills: knowledge of volcanoes and ability to use scientific equipment

education: advanced degree in geology

prior experience: field experience in the study of volcanoes is required

hourly schedule: varies; research hours are spent camping by a volcano and other hours are spent in labs documenting results

salary: as high as $90,000 per year

HELP WANTED

On May 18, 1980, volcanologist David Johnston was camping at Mount St. Helens in the state of Washington. He radioed to nearby headquarters in the city of Vancouver, British Columbia, Canada, "Vancouver, Vancouver, this is it!" Shortly after, Mount St. Helens erupted. Johnston and 56 others died.

Scientists who study volcanoes are familiar with **geology** and are called volcanologists. To do their jobs, volcanologists set up stations around volcanoes. These stations are like camps. The camps have scientific tools. Some tools measure gases coming from the volcano. Other tools measure earthquakes and crack formations. Active volcanoes all behave differently. Some make gassy smoke for years and never erupt. Others, like Mount St. Helens, seem to erupt out of nowhere.

Erupting volcanoes can be deadly. Entire cities can be destroyed. Volcanologists work hard to predict eruptions. They know their predictions could lessen damage and save lives.

geology—the study of minerals, rocks, and soil

In 1815 a volcanic eruption sent so much ash into the air there was no sunlight for months. Crops in countries all over the world failed, causing death and starvation.

BEARDER

Beard growing contests are held all over the world. Men enter the contests to win prizes. They hope their beards will win them dinner at a fancy restaurant, or better yet, fill their wallets with cash.

Every contest begins with a clean-shaven face. Then the men grow their beards. It takes months. They grow them right up until the day of judging.

Some bearders have their diets down to a science. They take vitamins like A, B, and E while growing their beards. The vitamins keep their skin cells healthy. Healthy skin cells allow their hair to grow strong and fast.

Just like athletes, serious bearders watch their diets year-round. They eat protein-rich foods like eggs and meat. They exercise regularly and try to avoid sickness. These habits give them a better chance at growing the winning whiskers every time they compete.

Beard Team USA was crowned overall champion at the 2009 World Beard and Moustache Championships. One American bearder named David Traver styled his beard to look like an Alaskan snowshoe.

Participants pose at the 2007 International Beard Championships in Schoemberg, Germany.

GLOSSARY

archaeologist (ar-kee-OL-uh-jist)—a person who learns about the past by digging up old buildings or objects and studying them

artifact (AR-tuh-fakt)—an object made by human beings, especially a tool or weapon used in the past

atmosphere (AT-muhss-feer)—the mixture of gases that surrounds the earth

biology (bye-AH-luh-jee)—the study of plant and animal life

blue hole (BLOO HOHL)—an underwater cave

conservationist (kon-sur-VAY-shun-ist)—someone who works to protect Earth's natural resources

domestic (doh-MES-tik)—living near or with human beings

endorphin (en-DOR-fin)—a chemical released by the brain that masks pain and triggers positive feelings

endangered (en-DAYN-juhrd—at risk of dying out

evidence (EV-uh-duhnss)—information, items, and facts that help prove something to be true or false

exotic (ek-ZAH-tik)—very different or unusual

extinct (ik-STINKT)—no longer living; an extinct animal is one that has died out, with no more of its kind

food additive (FOOD ADD-ih-tiv)—a substance added to food to enhance its flavor or appearance

geology (jee-AHL-uh-jee)—the study of minerals, rocks, and soil

habitat (HAB-uh-tat)—the natural place and conditions in which a plant or animal lives

meteorologist (mee-tee-ur-AWL-uh-jist)—a person who studies and predicts the weather

radar (RAY-dar)—a device that uses radio waves to track the locations of objects

serotonin (sehr-uh-TO-nin)—a chemical created by the human body that is responsible for maintaining mood balance

sleep disorder (SLEEP dis-OR-der)—a disturbance of the normal sleep pattern

suspect (SUHS-pekt)—a person who is thought to be guilty of a crime

tornado probe (tor-NAY-doh PROHB)—a portable weather station that collects tornado data where other instruments can't

READ MORE

Chambers, Catherine, and Emily Shuckburgh. *Polar Scientist.* The Coolest Jobs on the Planet. Chicago: Heinemann, 2015.

Rusch, Elizabeth. *Volcanoes and the Science of Saving Lives.* Scientists in the Field Series. New York: Houghton Mifflin Harcourt, 2013.

INTERNET SITES

FactHound offers a safe, fun way to find Internet sites related to this book. All of the sites on FactHound have been researched by our staff.

Here's all you do:

Visit *www.facthound.com*

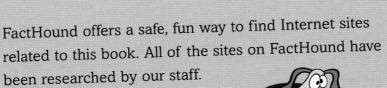

Type in this code: 9781491420317

CRITICAL THINKING USING THE COMMON CORE

1. Jobs such as storm chaser or animal trainer can be very dangerous. What other jobs might make workers put their lives on the line? (Integration of Knowledge and Ideas)

2. The "You'd Better Believe It!" fact on page 25 states that the average child laughs 400 times per day while the average adult laughs 15 times per day. Why do you think this is? What sorts of things might adults do in order to laugh more often? (Integration of Knowledge and Ideas)

INDEX